Sequencing Cut-Up Paragraphs

Find and Use Sequencing Cues to Understand, Organize, and Interpret "54" Fiction and Nonfiction Passages

by
Kelly Gunzenhauser

illustrated by
Ron Kaufmann

What did Lynn do at the pool?

Read the sentences. Cut them out and paste them in order so that the story makes sense.

Lynn took a new float out of the box.

She blew up the float until it was full, and the_____ the stopper.

Lynn climbed on the float and relaxed in the_____

What happened to Seth?

Read the sentences. Cut them out and paste them in order so that the story makes sense.

Seth fell off of his new, red bicycle.

He skinned his left knee and both of his hands.

Seth's dad gave him three bandages and a big hug.

What did Ryan see at the zoo?

Read the sentences. Cut them out and paste them in order so that the story makes sense.

First, Ryan saw the polar bears splash in the icy water.

_____an watched the monkeys swing through the

_____saw the lions nap in the tall grass.

_____n watched the seals jump in the pond.

Key Education
An imprint of Carson-Dellosa Publishing LLC
Greensboro, North Carolina

www.keyeducationpublishing.com

CONGRATULATIONS ON YOUR PURCHASE OF A KEY EDUCATION PRODUCT!

The editors at Key Education are former teachers who bring experience, enthusiasm, and quality to each and every product. Thousands of teachers have looked to the staff at Key Education for new and innovative resources to make their work more enjoyable and rewarding. Key Education is committed to developing and publishing educational materials that will assist teachers in building a strong and developmentally appropriate curriculum for young children.

PLAN FOR GREAT TEACHING EXPERIENCES WHEN YOU USE EDUCATIONAL MATERIALS FROM KEY EDUCATION PUBLISHING COMPANY, LLC

Credits
Authors: Kelly Gunzenhauser
Publisher: Sherrill B. Flora
Creative Director: Annette Hollister-Papp
Illustrator: Ron Kauffmann
Editor: Claude Chalk
Production: Key Education Staff
Cover Photo Credits: © Shutterstock.com

Dedication: For Drew and Garrett, my other two kids.

–KG

About the Author

Kelly Gunzenhauser has a master's degree in English and taught writing at the college level. She has worked in educational publishing for eleven years and is the author of five books for teachers and children, including Key Education's *Sequencing Cut-Up Paragraphs, Creating Curriculum Using Children's Picture Books, Reading for Details,* and *Let's Learn and Play!* Kelly has two sons in preschool and spends her time playing and learning with them, and volunteering at their school.

Key Education
An imprint of Carson-Dellosa Publishing LLC
PO Box 35665
Greensboro, NC 27425 USA
www.keyeducationpublishing.com

ISBN 978-1-602680-47-0
01-146148091

Table of Contents

Introduction

The hands-on reading activity of assembling "cut-up" or "mixed-up" sentences is a popular tool for teaching children to read. This approach is integrated into many reading philosophies and practices, including many prominent basal reading programs, the Reading Recovery® program, and the Four-Blocks® Literacy Model. You may even remember this activity from your own elementary school days. This time-tested theory has been proven to be both fun and effective. Learning to read while getting to cut and paste is a multi-sensory experience that helps meet the needs of children with different ability levels and learning styles.

Cut-up sentence activities also help children meet many of the national and state reading standards. When children participate in cut-up sentence activities, they will develop skills and strategies that will assist them in comprehending, evaluating, interpreting, and appreciating what they read. They will learn one-to-one correspondence between spoken and written words, left-to-right directionality, return sweep, uppercase letter recognition (as a cue for the beginnings of sentences), ending punctuation recognition, distinguishing letters from words, reading high-frequency words, connecting experiences to text, and using sentences to share information. Additionally, English Language Learners (ELL) will practice using common English sentence structures through cut-up sentence activities. Read ahead to find out how to use this fun and helpful resource.

Use whole group activities to introduce the concept of cut-up sentence sequencing.

1. Let each child complete the top half of the practice page (page 6) individually. Next, complete the bottom half as a class before working with sentence pages.
2. Choose one of the stories. Write each sentence from the story on a sentence strip.
3. Mix up the sentences. Place them in a pocket chart (out of order), fasten them to a bulletin board with tacks, or attach them to a chalkboard with magnets.
4. Read the sentences. Discuss whether the events could happen in the order in which you read them.
5. Let students tell you how the sentences should be ordered.
6. Either move the sentences during the discussion, or have volunteers come to the pocket chart to move the strips around.
7. Follow up by giving each child a copy of the story and letting them cut and paste the sentences.
8. When children are comfortable with the concept, rely on individual and small-group activities.

Individual Work

1. Give a copy of a story, a pair of safety scissors, and a glue stick to the child.
2. Help the child read the directional question, if necessary.
3. Tell each child to read all of the sentences, then cut them out.
4. The child should arrange the sentences in the correct order and paste each sentence within one of the guide boxes.
5. To create a more challenging activity, let the child glue the sentences onto a blank sheet. The child can either illustrate the individual sentences or draw a picture that represents the entire story.

Center Work

1. If copies are at a premium, make one copy of each page, cut out the directions, the sentences, and the illustration. Laminate all pieces.
2. Store each set of laminated pieces in a folder.
3. Label the outsides of the folders with the title question and the reading level. If you prefer not to reveal the reading level, use the Table of Contents as a master sheet.
4. At the center, have each child choose a folder, read the directions, look at the illustration, and put the sentences in order.

Assessment

Use this assessment to measure each student's progress utilizing cut-up sentence activities.

1. Choose a story that is at, or slightly below, each child's individual reading level.
2. Have the children work independently to put the sentences in order.
3. Have each child glue the sentences onto a piece of blank paper (no illustrations or grids).
4. After the glue is dry, have each child read the story to you.
5. Use the Mini-Assessment Grid found at the bottom of this page to document each child's performance.

Pictorial Assessment

You can also have children look at the sentences, then illustrate them in the correct order. Check to make sure the pictures are in the correct order. This can be effective practice for visual learners, as well.

- -

Mini-Assessment Grid	
Child's Name:	Date:
Story Title:	Level:
Number of sentences in the story. _____ Number of sentences in the correct order. _____	
Notes:	
Can the child explain why he/she pasted the sentences in the chosen order? Comments:	
Place a +, ✔ or – next to each characteristic for the read-aloud. Read high-frequency words fluently. _____ Used proper inflection for punctuation. _____ Maintained one-to-one correspondence. _____ Was able to retell the story in his/her own words. _____	

Practice Page: Key Words

Directions: Sometimes words in a story can help you find out the sequence of what happened. Look at the first group of words. Draw a line from each word to its matching number.

Third	**2**
First	**3**
Fifth	**4**
Fourth	**1**
Second	**5**

Directions: Use this fill-in-the-blank activity to familiarize children with words that will help them sequence sentences. Make a transparency of the story below. Read each sentence aloud and help children decide which word from the word list to write in the blank. As an extra activity, let children name synonyms for some of the words.

Finally	Then	Next	Last	Later	Beginning	First	End	Before

Joy wanted to make a cake. _____, she found a good recipe. She _____ measured the sugar and butter. _____ she started mixing them, she added two eggs. The _____ thing she added was flour. She added just a little flour at the _____ of the mixing time. At the _____ she added the rest. Her _____ ingredients were salt, baking powder, and flavoring. _____, her cake was ready to bake. One hour _____, she pulled it out of the oven. Yummy!

✂ -

Answer Key

Joy wanted to make a cake. First, she found a good recipe. She then measured the sugar and butter. Before she started mixing them, she added two eggs. The next thing she added was flour. She added just a little flour at the beginning of the mixing time. At the end she added the rest. Her last ingredients were salt, baking powder, and flavoring. Finally, her cake was ready to bake. One hour later, she pulled it out of the oven. Yummy!

What happened to Seth?

Read the sentences. Cut them out and paste them in order so that the story makes sense.

glue here

glue here

glue here

Seth's dad gave him three bandages and a big hug.

Seth fell off of his new red bicycle.

He skinned his left knee and both of his hands.

What happened when Mary missed the school bus?

Read the sentences. Cut them out and paste them in order so that the story makes sense.

glue here

glue here

glue here

Mary asked her mom to drive her to school in their car.

Mary ran from the bus stop back to her house.

Mary's mom drove Mary to school.

Name _____

What did Emma eat for breakfast?

Read the sentences. Cut them out and paste them in order so that the story makes sense.

glue here

glue here

glue here

glue here

 -

Emma ate them with juice and fruit.

Her dad cracked the eggs into a pan.

Emma wanted eggs for breakfast.

He scrambled the eggs.

Why is Nate all wet?

Read the sentences. Cut them out and paste them in order so that the story makes sense.

> *glue here*

> *glue here*

> *glue here*

> *glue here*

Nate's brother Owen picked up the hose.

Nate used the hose when he washed his mother's new car.

He forgot to turn off the hose.

Owen soaked Nate with the hose.

What is the best way to fold a shirt?

Read the sentences. Cut them out and paste them in order so that the story makes sense.

glue here
glue here
glue here
glue here
glue here
glue here

✄ -

Fold back the sleeves so that they are even with the sides of the shirt.

Lay the shirt facedown.

Fold the sleeve and bottom to the center of the shirt.

Pick up one sleeve and the bottom of the shirt.

Fold the shirt twice, from the bottom up.

Fold the other side in the same way.

What did Kylie do for her birthday?

Read the sentences. Cut them out and paste them in order so that the story makes sense.

glue here

glue here

glue here

glue here

✂ -

They skated for two hours.

Kylie and her mom picked up her friends Maddie and Mercer.

When they got tired, they went to the snack bar.

Kylie's mom drove them to the roller skating rink.

Where does Joey go on his snowshoes?

Read the sentences. Cut them out and paste them in order so that the story makes sense.

> glue here

> glue here

> glue here

> glue here

✂ -

Next, Joey milks the sleepy cows.

First, he walks to the barn and feeds hay to the horses.

Every morning, Joey puts on his snowshoes.

Last, Joey gives some fresh milk to the cats.

What kind of haircut will Chase get?

Read the sentences. Cut them out and paste them in order so that the story makes sense.

glue here

glue here

glue here

glue here

glue here

✂ -

Chase hopes it will grow back soon!

He goes to the barbershop.

Chase wants a new kind of haircut.

He asks the barber for a buzz cut.

The barber uses clippers to shave off Chase's hair.

Why does Hattie's scout troop build a fire?

Read the sentences. Cut them out and paste them in order so that the story makes sense.

glue here

glue here

glue here

glue here

glue here

glue here

✂ -

Next, they gather wood for the fire.

They put the small sticks on the bottom.

They light the fire and roast hot dogs over the fire.

They use water to put out the fire safely when they are finished eating.

First, Hattie's scout troop clears a space for the fire.

They put logs on top of the sticks.

How did Mrs. Brown fix her tire?

Read the sentences. Cut them out and paste them in order so that the story makes sense.

glue here

glue here

glue here

glue here

glue here

glue here

✂ -

Mrs. Brown tightened the lug nuts, lowered the car, and drove off.

After she lifted the car, she pulled off the flat tire.

Mrs. Brown's car ran over a nail and got a flat tire.

Next, she used the jack to lift the car.

First, she loosened the lug nuts on the tire.

She put on the new tire, and then put the flat tire in the trunk.

What did Noel send to his friend?

Read the sentences. Cut them out and paste them in order so that the story makes sense.

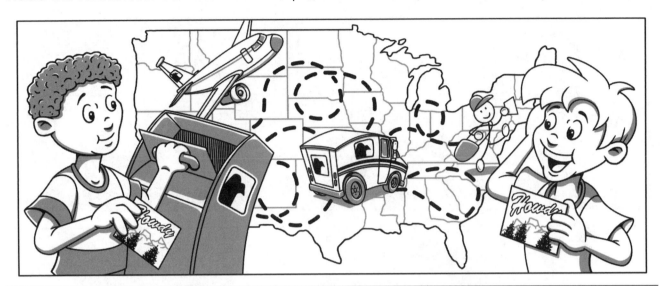

glue here

glue here

glue here

✂ -

He put the postcard in the mailbox.

He put a stamp on the postcard.

Noel wrote a postcard to his friend Trey in Boston.

What chore does Viv do for her dog?

Read the sentences. Cut them out and paste them in order so that the story makes sense.

glue here

glue here

glue here

glue here

✂ -

Then, she puts the pillows on top of the blanket.

When Viv is finished, her dog jumps on the bed to sleep.

First, Viv pulls up the sheet.

Next, she pulls up the blanket.

KE-804068 © Key Education -18- *Sequencing Cut-Up Paragraphs*

Name

How do you draw a pig?

Read the sentences. Cut them out and paste them in order so that the story makes sense.

glue here

glue here

glue here

glue here

Last, add a mouth and eyes to the pig's face.

Add an oval for the snout and triangles for the legs.

Draw two ovals for the pig's head and body.

Draw on ears, a tail, and hooves.

KE-804068 © Key Education =-19-= *Sequencing Cut-Up Paragraphs*

Name

Why did Will wash his dog?

Read the sentences. Cut them out and paste them in order so that the story makes sense.

glue here

glue here

glue here

glue here

✂ ---------------------------------

The skunk ran away after it sprayed Pal.

Will's dog Pal ran under the porch and scared a skunk.

Will washed Pal with dog shampoo, but Pal still smelled terrible.

The skunk sprayed Pal and made Pal stink!

What exciting thing did Jade do?

Read the sentences. Cut them out and paste them in order so that the story makes sense.

glue here

glue here

glue here

glue here

glue here

✂ -

Jade climbed up the tall ladder.

She made a huge splash at the bottom of the slide!

She pushed herself down the water slide.

Jade slid through the tunnel and around the sharp curves.

She sat down on a squishy mat.

What did Sam do over spring break?

Read the sentences. Cut them out and paste them in order so that the story makes sense.

glue here

glue here

glue here

glue here

✂ -

On Tuesday and Wednesday, she played in the rain with her friend Ben.

On Monday, Sam taught her dog some tricks.

On Friday, Sam went to the park.

Sam got sick and had to stay in bed on Thursday.

What did Ryan see at the zoo?

glue here

glue here

glue here

glue here

✂

Fourth, Ryan watched the seals jump in the pond.

Second, Ryan watched the monkeys swing through the trees.

First, Ryan saw the polar bears splash in the icy water.

Third, Ryan saw the lions nap in the tall grass.

How can you make a birdhouse?

Read the sentences. Cut them out and paste them in order so that the story makes sense.

glue here

glue here

glue here

glue here

glue here

✂--

Ask an adult to help you cover the gourd with shellac, then let it dry.

Wrap wire around the gourd and hang it from a tree branch.

Shake the gourd seeds out of the hole.

Find a dried gourd with a long neck.

Have an adult cut a round hole in the side of the gourd.

How do you make a face sandwich?

Read the sentences. Cut them out and paste them in order so that the story makes sense.

glue here

glue here

glue here

glue here

glue here

glue here

✂ -

Under the nose, fold a slice of lunchmeat to make a mouth.

Spread cream cheese on the bread.

First, put a piece of bread on a plate.

Under the eyes, add a pickle nose.

Add some shredded lettuce hair and enjoy!

Cut a green olive in half and use the halves for eyes.

Can Carson learn a new trick?

Read the sentences. Cut them out and paste them in order so that the story makes sense.

glue here

glue here

glue here

glue here

glue here

glue here

He climbs up and walks to the end of the diving board.

Carson walks up to the ladder.

Slowly, he falls forward and rolls in the air.

Carson bends over to touch his toes.

Carson is proud of doing his very first flip!

He lands in the water feet first.

What did Lynn do at the pool?

Read the sentences. Cut them out and paste them in order so that the story makes sense.

glue here

glue here

glue here

Lynn took a new float out of the box.

Lynn climbed on the float and relaxed in the pool.

She blew up the float until it was full, and then closed the stopper.

     Sequencing Cut-Up Paragraphs

What did Drew win?

Read the sentences. Cut them out and paste them in order so that the story makes sense.

glue here

glue here

glue here

glue here

✂ -

He covered it with cream cheese frosting.

Drew's cake won first prize!

Drew baked a pound cake.

He entered it into the county fair baking contest.

How did Tom do in his race?

Read the sentences. Cut them out and paste them in order so that the story makes sense.

glue here

glue here

glue here

glue here

✂ -

Tom got into his soapbox derby car.

Tom crossed the finish line in first place.

He rolled away from the starting line.

He passed the other cars.

How does a frog grow?

Read the sentences. Cut them out and paste them in order so that the story makes sense.

glue here

glue here

glue here

glue here

glue here

✂ -

Their tails disappear after they grow legs.

A mother frog lays eggs in the water.

The tadpoles soon grow legs, and they grow lungs to breathe air.

Tadpoles hatch from the eggs.

They turn into adult frogs.

What can a bird do with a snake's skin?

Read the sentences. Cut them out and paste them in order so that the story makes sense.

glue here

glue here

glue here

glue here

glue here

Rubbing against a rough surface tears a small hole in the skin.

The snake rubs its nose against the rough object.

When a bird finds the skin, it may use the skin to build a nest.

The snake crawls and wiggles out of the old skin.

To shed its skin, the snake finds a rough tree or rock.

What stinky job does Jill have to do?

Read the sentences. Cut them out and paste them in order so that the story makes sense.

glue here

glue here

glue here

glue here

✂ -

First, Jill scoops the dirty cat litter into a trash bag.

Last, she throws away the trash bag.

Then, Jill puts clean litter in the cat's litter box.

Jill has to clean out the cat's yucky litter box.

What is Carlos helping his mom do with those shirts?

Read the sentences. Cut them out and paste them in order so that the story makes sense.

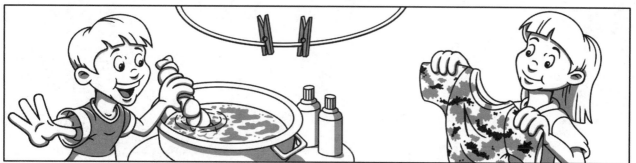

glue here

glue here

glue here

glue here

glue here

✂ -

Now they have two cool shirts!

Carlos dipped the T-shirts into red and yellow dye.

Carlos and his mom bought two white T-shirts.

When the shirts were full of rubber bands, Carlos's mom mixed some dye.

Carlos wrapped lots of rubber bands around the shirts.

Where can Dean find buried treasure?

Read the sentences. Cut them out and paste them in order so that the story makes sense.

glue here

glue here

glue here

glue here

glue here

✂ -

From the stairs, Dean must walk ten steps to the big sand dune.

He has to dig two feet deep under the very crooked palm tree.

Dean must climb the dune and look for the very crooked palm tree.

After Dean finds the buried treasure, he will share it with his friend.

First, Dean must stand on his porch stairs.

What is that sticky stuff?

Read the sentences. Cut them out and paste them in order so that the story makes sense.

glue here

glue here

glue here

glue here

glue here

glue here

✂ -

Leo wanted to know what made the sticky stuff.

Leo saw some shiny stuff on the ground.

It felt sticky.

He touched it.

He followed the sticky, shiny trail to a big leaf.

He found a slimy slug under the leaf.

What did Lily find in the garden?

Read the sentences. Cut them out and paste them in order so that the story makes sense.

glue here

glue here

glue here

glue here

glue here

glue here

She pulled up a lot of weeds.

Lily went out to work in her garden.

The blisters started to itch.

The next day, she got some blisters on her hands.

Lily's mom said that Lily had poison ivy!

Her mom looked at the itchy blisters.

Why did Mia sit down with a bang?

Read the sentences. Cut them out and paste them in order so that the story makes sense.

> glue here

> glue here

> glue here

> glue here

✂ -

First, she squeezed it with her hands.

- -

Next, she tried jumping on the balloon, but she fell off.

- -

At last, she sat on her balloon and it made a big bang!

- -

Silly Mia wanted to pop her blue balloon.

Can Ken catch all of the pennies?

Read the sentences. Cut them out and paste them in order so that the story makes sense.

glue here

glue here

glue here

glue here

First, Ken touched his shoulder with his hand and held up his elbow.

Next, Ken will try the same trick with six pennies.

Quickly, Ken threw out his hand and caught all five pennies.

Then, he stacked five pennies on his elbow.

Will Zane take a fall?

Read the sentences. Cut them out and paste them in order so that the story makes sense.

glue here

glue here

glue here

glue here

glue here

✄ -

He slid away from the starting line.

He jumped off a big hill and tried a back flip.

Zane carried his board back to the starting line to try again.

Zane strapped on his snowboard.

Zane did not flip fast enough and landed on his belly in the snow.

What did Ava grow?

Read the sentences. Cut them out and paste them in order so that the story makes sense.

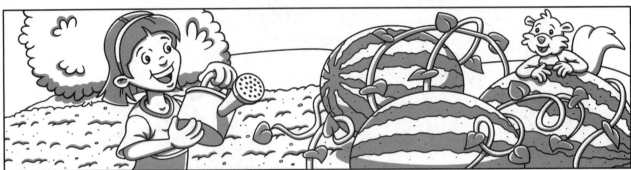

glue here

glue here

glue here

glue here

glue here

✂ -

Ava bought some seeds at the garden store.

Tiny fruit grew on the vines.

She planted the seeds.

The fruit grew into big watermelons!

The seeds grew into vines.

Did Ella keep the other team from scoring?

Read the sentences. Cut them out and paste them in order so that the story makes sense.

glue here

glue here

glue here

She caught it before it went into the goal.

She threw the ball back to her teammates.

Ella got ready to block the soccer ball.

Name

What does David like on his pizza?

Read the sentences. Cut them out and paste them in order so that the story makes sense.

glue here

glue here

glue here

glue here

He bakes the pizza until the cheese melts.

He puts tomato sauce and peppers on the crust.

He covers the sauce with cheese.

David puts a plain pizza crust on a pan.

What kind of insect hides to eat?

Read the sentences. Cut them out and paste them in order so that the story makes sense.

glue here

glue here

glue here

glue here

glue here

A small cricket jumps and lands near the mantis.

The mantis grabs the cricket.

It folds up its front legs and waits.

The praying mantis eats its lunch.

The praying mantis hides in some leaves.

What does Jo do each day at camp?

Read the sentences. Cut them out and paste them in order so that the story makes sense.

glue here

glue here

glue here

glue here

glue here

glue here

✂ -

Jo reads after dinner.

Jo takes a hike in the woods after eating breakfast.

Jo swims in the lake after her ride.

Jo goes to bed by 9:00.

She has dinner after her swim.

She rides a horse on the trail after lunch.

What food can you make with a marble?

Read the sentences. Cut them out and paste them in order so that the story makes sense.

glue here

glue here

glue here

glue here

glue here

glue here

Put the lid on the jar and tighten it.

Pour a cup of heavy cream into a glass jar.

Add a marble and a little salt to the cream.

Open the jar and spread the tasty butter on some bread.

When the cream gets very thick, it has become butter!

Shake the closed jar for at least half an hour.

What will Liz do after school?

Read the sentences. Cut them out and paste them in order so that the story makes sense.

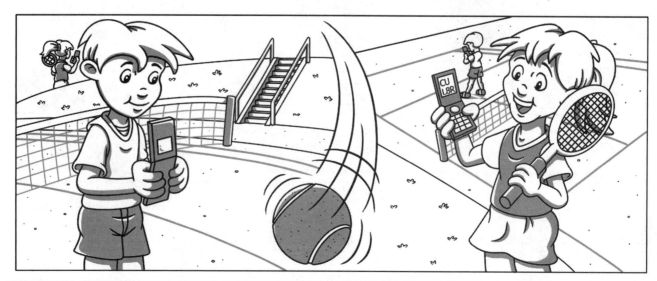

glue here

glue here

glue here

He asked Liz to bring her tennis racket to the park.

Evan sent a text message to Liz on her cell phone.

They played tennis after school.

What did Tyra do on her mom's computer?

Read the sentences. Cut them out and paste them in order so that the story makes sense.

glue here

glue here

glue here

✂ -

She clicked the "Send" button.

Tyra asked him to pick her up at school.

Tyra e-mailed her grandpa this morning.

What has eight legs and lives in a hole in the ground?

Read the sentences. Cut them out and paste them in order so that the story makes sense.

glue here

glue here

glue here

glue here

✂ -

They use dirt and a web to make a hidden door for the hole.

She drags the bug into the hole and has lunch!

When the spider feels a bug outside, she rushes out to grab it.

Trapdoor spiders live in holes in the ground.

Name _____

How does Zoe paint flowers on her toenails?

Read the sentences. Cut them out and paste them in order so that the story makes sense.

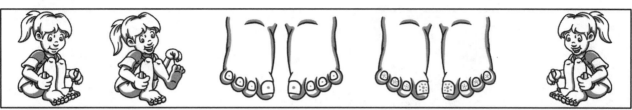

glue here

glue here

glue here

glue here

glue here

glue here

✂ -

She waits until the pink polish is dry.

Zoe paints her toenails with pink polish.

She makes a blue dot on her big toenail.

Zoe sticks a toothpick into blue nail polish.

When the flower is dry, Zoe paints clear polish on top.

She makes smaller blue dots around the first dot.

KE-804068 © Key Education ——————— -49- ——————— *Sequencing Cut-Up Paragraphs*

How can you make it to home plate?

Read the sentences. Cut them out and paste them in order so that the story makes sense.

glue here
glue here
glue here
glue here
glue here
glue here

✂ -

After you kick the ball as hard as you can, it's time to run the bases.

If the ball is still in the outfield, dash around to third base.

If the other team does not have the ball, sprint to second base.

Run from third base to home plate if you think you can make it.

Run from home plate to first base.

Congratulations on your home run!

How do you make your own bubbles?

Read the sentences. Cut them out and paste them in order so that the story makes sense.

glue here

glue here

glue here

Dip a bubble wand in the tub to blow bubbles.

Find a small, plastic tub with a lid.

Pour in two cups of dish soap, a cup of corn syrup, and a cup of water.

How did Sara get her film back?

Read the sentences. Cut them out and paste them in order so that the story makes sense.

glue here

glue here

glue here

glue here

- -

The horse picked up the film in its mouth.

Sara took a picture of a tall horse.

Sara opened the horse's mouth and pulled out the slimy film.

She took the film out of the camera and dropped it.

Does Rex finish the course?

Read the sentences. Cut them out and paste them in order so that the story makes sense.

glue here

glue here

glue here

glue here

✂ -

Rex leapt through the tire and then crossed the finish line.

After he was finished with the tunnel, Rex raced through the poles.

Next, he scooted through the tunnel as fast as he could.

First, Rex ran up the ramp and dashed down the other side.

What amazing thing can a sea star (starfish) do?

Read the sentences. Cut them out and paste them in order so that the story makes sense.

glue here

glue here

glue here

glue here

✂ -

Soon, a new leg grows in place of the lost one.

When it is attacked, a sea star can lose a leg.

Later, the lost leg may even turn into a brand new sea star!

Some animals attack sea stars and try to eat them.

Do you know how to ride a bike without training wheels?

Read the sentences. Cut them out and paste them in order so that the story makes sense.

glue here

glue here

glue here

glue here

glue here

✂ -

Get on the bike and ask an adult to hold onto the back.

Before you ride, make sure you have a helmet.

When you are going fast enough, have the adult let go of the bike.

When you need to stop, be sure to put your foot down first.

Start pedaling and balance on the wheels.

What will Meg and Jen build?

Read the sentences. Cut them out and paste them in order so that the story makes sense.

glue here

glue here

glue here

glue here

✂ -

Next, Jen threw a blanket over the chairs.

First, Meg put two kitchen chairs in the living room.

Meg and Jen wanted to build a fabulous fort.

They crawled inside the fort to read books and play games.

Name _____

What did Macy make for her sister?

Read the sentences. Cut them out and paste them in order so that the story makes sense.

glue here

glue here

glue here

glue here

glue here

 -

She tied the ends of the string together.

Macy picked out some glass beads.

She wrapped the bracelet and gave it to her sister.

Macy's sister loved her new bracelet.

She strung the beads on a stretchy string.

What kept Matt up all night?

Read the sentences. Cut them out and paste them in order so that the story makes sense.

glue here

glue here

glue here

glue here

glue here

glue here

✂ -

At breakfast, Matt decided to name his kitten Dawn.

At bedtime, Matt put the kitten in a basket.

She jumped out of the basket.

Matt got a new kitten at his birthday dinner.

She played on Matt's bed and kept him awake all night.

Matt hopes that Dawn will sleep tonight!

Did Audrey win the talent contest?

Read the sentences. Cut them out and paste them in order so that the story makes sense.

glue here

glue here

glue here

glue here

glue here

✂ -

She played two songs on her violin.

When it was her turn, she walked on stage.

Audrey entered the talent contest at school.

Audrey won first place and got a big trophy!

The audience clapped loudly when she finished.

How do robins make their nest?

Read the sentences. Cut them out and paste them in order so that the story makes sense.

glue here

glue here

glue here

glue here

glue here

glue here

✂ -

Robins find a safe place to build their nest.

The female weaves the grasses and twigs together.

They gather hundreds of twigs and pieces of grass.

The female sits on the nest to make a space for her eggs.

She uses mud to help hold the twigs together.

The mud also helps stick the nest to the tree.

Answer Key

Page 7 – What happened to Seth?
1. Seth fell off of his new red bicycle.
2. He skinned his left knee and both of his hands.
3. Seth's dad gave him three bandages and a big hug.

Page 8 – What happened when Mary missed the school bus?
1. Mary ran from the bus stop back to her house.
2. Mary asked her mom to drive her to school in their car.
3. Mary's mom drove Mary to school.

Page 9 – What did Emma eat for breakfast?
1. Emma wanted eggs for breakfast.
2. Her dad cracked the eggs into a pan.
3. He scrambled the eggs.
4. Emma ate them with juice and fruit.

Page 10 – Why is Nate all wet?
1. Nate used the hose when he washed his mother's new car.
2. He forgot to turn off the hose.
3. Nate's brother Owen picked up the hose.
4. Owen soaked Nate with the hose.

Page 11 – What is the best way to fold a shirt?
1. Lay the shirt facedown.
2. Fold back the sleeves so that they are even with the sides of the shirt.
3. Pick up one sleeve and the bottom of the shirt.
4. Fold the sleeve and bottom to the center of the shirt.
5. Fold the other side in the same way.
6. Fold the shirt twice, from the bottom up.

Page 12 – What did Kylie do for her birthday?
1. Kylie and her mom picked up her friends Maddie and Mercer.
2. Kylie's mom drove them to the roller skating rink.
3. They skated for two hours.
4. When they got tired, they went to the snack bar.

Page 13 – Where does Joey go on his snowshoes?
1. Every morning, Joey puts on his snowshoes.
2. First, he walks to the barn and feeds hay to the horses.
3. Next, Joey milks the sleepy cows.
4. Last, Joey gives some fresh milk to the cats.

Page 14 – What kind of haircut will Chase get?
1. Chase wants a new kind of haircut.
2. He goes to the barbershop.
3. He asks the barber for a buzz cut.
4. The barber uses clippers to shave off Chase's hair.
5. Chase hopes it will grow back soon!

Page 15 – Why does Hattie's scout troop build a fire?
1. First, Hattie's scout troop clears a space for the fire.
2. Next, they gather wood for the fire.
3. They put the small sticks on the bottom.
4. They put logs on top of the sticks.
5. They light the fire and roast hot dogs over the fire.
6. They use water to put out the fire safely when they are finished eating.

Page 16 – How did Mrs. Brown fix her tire?
1. Mrs. Brown's car ran over a nail and got a flat tire.
2. First, she loosened the lug nuts on the tire.
3. Next, she used the jack to lift the car.
4. After she lifted the car, she pulled off the flat tire.
5. She put on the new tire, and then put the flat tire in the trunk.
6. Mrs. Brown tightened the lug nuts, lowered the car, and drove off.

Page 17 – What did Noel send to his friend?
1. Noel wrote a postcard to his friend Trey in Boston.
2. He put a stamp on the postcard.
3. He put the postcard in the mailbox.

Page 18 – What chore does Viv do for her dog?
1. First, Viv pulls up the sheet.
2. Next, she pulls up the blanket.
3. Then, she puts the pillows on top of the blanket.
4. When Viv is finished, her dog jumps on the bed to sleep.

Page 19 – How do you draw a pig?
1. Draw two ovals for the pig's head and body.
2. Add an oval for the snout and triangles for the legs.
3. Draw on ears, a tail, and hooves.
4. Last, add a mouth and eyes to the pig's face.

Page 20 – Why did Will wash his dog?
1. Will's dog Pal ran under the porch and scared a skunk.
2. The skunk sprayed Pal and made Pal stink!
3. The skunk ran away after it sprayed Pal.
4. Will washed Pal with dog shampoo, but Pal still smelled terrible.

Page 21 – What exciting thing did Jade do?
1. Jade climbed up the tall ladder.
2. She sat down on a squishy mat.
3. She pushed herself down the water slide.
4. Jade slid through the tunnel and around the sharp curves.
5. She made a huge splash at the bottom of the slide!

Page 22 – What did Sam do over spring break?
1. On Monday, Sam taught her dog some tricks.
2. On Tuesday and Wednesday, she played in the rain with her friend Ben.
3. Sam got sick and had to stay in bed on Thursday.
4. On Friday, Sam went to the park.

Page 23 – What did Ryan see at the zoo?
1. First, Ryan saw the polar bears splash in the icy water.
2. Second, Ryan watched the monkeys swing through the trees.
3. Third, Ryan saw the lions nap in the tall grass.
4. Fourth, Ryan watched the seals jump in the pond.

Page 24 – How can you make a birdhouse?
1. Find a dried gourd with a long neck.
2. Have an adult cut a round hole in the side of the gourd.
3. Shake the gourd seeds out of the hole.
4. Ask an adult to help you cover the gourd with shellac, then let it dry.
5. Wrap wire around the gourd and hang it from a tree branch.

Page 25 – How do you make a face sandwich?
1. First, put a piece of bread on a plate.
2. Spread cream cheese on the bread.
3. Cut a green olive in half and use the halves for eyes.
4. Under the eyes, add a pickle nose.
5. Under the nose, fold a slice of lunchmeat to make a mouth.
6. Add some shredded lettuce hair and enjoy!

Page 26 – Can Carson learn a new trick?
1. Carson walks up to the ladder.
2. He climbs up and walks to the end of the diving board.
3. Carson bends over to touch his toes.
4. Slowly, he falls forward and rolls in the air.
5. He lands in the water feet first.
6. Carson is proud of doing his very first flip!

Page 27 – What did Lynn do at the pool?
1. Lynn took a new float out of the box.
2. She blew up the float until it was full, and then closed the stopper.
3. Lynn climbed on the float and relaxed in the pool.

Page 28 – What did Drew win?
1. Drew baked a pound cake.
2. He covered it with cream cheese frosting.
3. He entered it into the county fair baking contest.
4. Drew's cake won first prize!

Page 29 – How did Tom do in his race?
1. Tom got into his soapbox derby car.
2. He rolled away from the starting line.
3. He passed the other cars.
4. Tom crossed the finish line in first place.

Page 30 – How does a frog grow?
1. A mother frog lays eggs in the water.
2. Tadpoles hatch from the eggs.
3. The tadpoles soon grow legs, and they grow lungs to breathe air.
4. Their tails disappear after they grow legs.
5. They turn into adult frogs.

Page 31 – What can a bird do with a snake's skin?
1. To shed its skin, the snake finds a rough tree or rock.
2. The snake rubs its nose against the rough object.
3. Rubbing against a rough surface tears a small hole in the skin.
4. The snake crawls and wiggles out of the old skin.
5. When a bird finds the skin, it may use the skin to build a nest.

Page 32 – What stinky job does Jill have to do?
1. Jill has to clean out the cat's yucky litter box.
2. First, Jill scoops the dirty cat litter into a trash bag.
3. Then, Jill puts clean litter in the cat's litter box.
4. Last, she throws away the trash bag.

Page 33 – What is Carlos helping his mom do with those shirts?
1. Carlos and his mom bought two white T-shirts.
2. Carlos wrapped lots of rubber bands around the shirts.
3. When the shirts were full of rubber bands, Carlos's mom mixed some dye.
4. Carlos dipped the T-shirts into red and yellow dye.
5. Now they have two cool shirts!

Page 34 – Where can Dean find buried treasure?
1. First, Dean must stand on his porch stairs.
2. From the stairs, Dean must walk ten steps to the big sand dune.
3. Dean must climb the dune and look for the very crooked palm tree.
4. He has to dig two feet deep under the very crooked palm tree.
5. After Dean finds the buried treasure, he will share it with his friend.

Page 35 – What is that sticky stuff?
1. Leo saw some shiny stuff on the ground.
2. He touched it.
3. It felt sticky.
4. Leo wanted to know what made the sticky stuff.
5. He followed the sticky, shiny trail to a big leaf.
6. He found a slimy slug under the leaf.

Page 36 – What did Lily find in the garden?
1. Lily went out to work in her garden.
2. She pulled up a lot of weeds.
3. The next day, she got some blisters on her hands.
4. The blisters started to itch.
5. Her mom looked at the itchy blisters.
6. Lily's mom said that Lily had poison ivy!

Page 37 – Why did Mia sit down with a bang?
1. Silly Mia wanted to pop her blue balloon.
2. First, she squeezed it with her hands.
3. Next, she tried jumping on the balloon, but she fell off.
4. At last, she sat on her balloon and it made a big bang!

Page 38 – Can Ken catch all of the pennies?
1. First, Ken touched his shoulder with his hand and held up his elbow.
2. Then, he stacked five pennies on his elbow.
3. Quickly, Ken threw out his hand and caught all five pennies.
4. Next, Ken will try the same trick with six pennies.

Page 39 – Will Zane take a fall?
1. Zane strapped on his snowboard.
2. He slid away from the starting line.
3. He jumped off a big hill and tried a back flip.
4. Zane did not flip fast enough and landed on his belly in the snow.
5. Zane carried his board back to the starting line to try again.

Page 40 – What did Ava grow?
1. Ava bought some seeds at the garden store.
2. She planted the seeds.
3. The seeds grew into vines.
4. Tiny fruit grew on the vines.
5. The fruit grew into big watermelons!

Page 41 – Did Ella keep the other team from scoring?
1. Ella got ready to block the soccer ball.
2. She caught it before it went into the goal.
3. She threw the ball back to her teammates.

Page 42 – What does David like on his pizza?
1. David puts a plain pizza crust on a pan.
2. He puts tomato sauce and peppers on the crust.
3. He covers the sauce with cheese.
4. He bakes the pizza until the cheese melts.

Page 43 – What kind of insect hides to eat?
1. The praying mantis hides in some leaves.
2. It folds up its front legs and waits.
3. A small cricket jumps and lands near the mantis.
4. The mantis grabs the cricket.
5. The praying mantis eats its lunch.

Page 44 – What does Jo do each day at camp?
1. Jo takes a hike in the woods after eating breakfast.
2. She rides a horse on the trail after lunch.
3. Jo swims in the lake after her ride.
4. She has dinner after her swim.
5. Jo reads after dinner.
6. Jo goes to bed by 9:00.

Page 45 – What food can you make with a marble?
1. Pour a cup of heavy cream into a glass jar.
2. Add a marble and a little salt to the cream.
3. Put the lid on the jar and tighten it.
4. Shake the closed jar for at least half an hour.
5. When the cream gets very thick, it has become butter!
6. Open the jar and spread the tasty butter on some bread.

Page 46 – What will Liz do after school?
1. Evan sent a text message to Liz on her cell phone.
2. He asked Liz to bring her tennis racket to the park.
3. They played tennis after school.

Page 47 – What did Tyra do on her mom's computer?
1. Tyra e-mailed her grandpa this morning.
2. Tyra asked him to pick her up at school.
3. She clicked the "Send" button.

Page 48 – What has eight legs and lives in a hole in the ground?
1. Trapdoor spiders live in holes in the ground.
2. They use dirt and a web to make a hidden door for the hole.
3. When the spider feels a bug outside, she rushes out to grab it.
4. She drags the bug into the hole and has lunch!

Page 49 – How does Zoe paint flowers on her toenails?
1. Zoe paints her toenails with pink polish.
2. She waits until the pink polish is dry.
3. She makes a blue dot on her big toenail.
4. Zoe sticks a toothpick into blue nail polish.
5. She makes smaller blue dots around the first dot.
6. When the flower is dry, Zoe paints clear polish on top.

Page 50 – How can you make it to home plate?
1. After you kick the ball as hard as you can, it's time to run the bases.
2. Run from home plate to first base.
3. If the other team does not have the ball, sprint to second base.
4. If the ball is still in the outfield, dash around to third base.
5. Run from third base to home plate if you think you can make it.
6. Congratulations on your home run!

Page 51 – How do you make your own bubbles?
1. Find a small, plastic tub with a lid.
2. Pour in two cups of dish soap, a cup of corn syrup, and a cup of water.
3. Dip a bubble wand in the tub to blow bubbles.

Page 52 – How did Sara get her film back?
1. Sara took a picture of a tall horse.
2. She took the film out of the camera and dropped it.
3. The horse picked up the film in its mouth.
4. Sara opened the horse's mouth and pulled out the slimy film.

Page 53 – Does Rex finish the course?
1. First, Rex ran up the ramp and dashed down the other side.
2. Next, he scooted through the tunnel as fast as he could.
3. After he was finished with the tunnel, Rex raced through the poles.
4. Rex leapt through the tire and then crossed the finish line.

Page 54 – What amazing thing can a sea star (starfish) do?
1. Some animals attack sea stars and try to eat them.
2. When it is attacked, a sea star can lose a leg.
3. Soon, a new leg grows in place of the lost one.
4. Later, the lost leg may even turn into a brand new sea star!

Page 55 – Do you know how to ride a bike without training wheels?
1. Before you ride, make sure you have a helmet.
2. Get on the bike and ask an adult to hold onto the back.
3. Start pedaling and balance on the wheels.
4. When you are going fast enough, have the adult let go of the bike.
5. When you need to stop, be sure to put your foot down first.

Page 56 – What will Meg and Jen build?
1. Meg and Jen wanted to build a fabulous fort.
2. First, Meg put the kitchen chairs in the living room.
3. Next, Jen threw a blanket over the chairs.
4. They crawled inside the fort to read books and play games.

Page 57 – What did Macy make for her sister?
1. Macy picked out some glass beads.
2. She strung the beads on a stretchy string.
3. She tied the ends of the string together.
4. She wrapped the bracelet and gave it to her sister.
5. Macy's sister loved her new bracelet.

Page 58 – What kept Matt up all night?
1. Matt got a new kitten at his birthday dinner.
2. At bedtime, Matt put the kitten in a basket.
3. She jumped out of the basket.
4. She played on Matt's bed and kept him awake all night.
5. At breakfast, Matt decided to name his kitten Dawn.
6. Matt hopes that Dawn will sleep tonight!

Page 59 – Did Audrey win the talent contest?
1. Audrey entered the talent contest at school.
2. When it was her turn, she walked on stage.
3. She played two songs on her violin.
4. The audience clapped loudly when she finished.
5. Audrey won first place and got a big trophy!

Page 60 – How do robins make their nest?
1. Robins find a safe place to build their nest.
2. They gather hundreds of twigs and pieces of grass.
3. The female weaves the grasses and twigs together.
4. She uses mud to help hold the twigs together.
5. The mud also helps stick the nest to the tree.
6. The female sits on the nest to make a space for her eggs.

Correlations to the Standards

This book supports the NCTE/IRA Standards for the English Language Arts, the recommended teaching practices outlined in the NAEYC/IRA position statement Learning to Read and Write: Developmentally Appropriate Practices for Young Children, and the National Science Education Standards.

────────────────── NCTE/IRA Standards for the English Language Arts ──────────────────

Each activity in this book supports one or more of the following standards:

1. **Students read many different types of print and nonprint texts for a variety of purposes.** To do the activities in *Sequencing Cut-Up Paragraphs*, students must read fiction and nonfiction passages plus the illustrations that go along with them.

2. **Students use a variety of strategies to build meaning while reading.** The main strategy taught in *Sequencing Cut-Up Paragraphs* is sequencing, but the activities in it also support one-to-one correspondence, directionality, sentence recognition, high frequency words, vocabulary, inference, and other comprehension skills and strategies.

3. **Students communicate in spoken, written, and visual form, for a variety of purposes and a variety of audiences.** Students communicate in spoken and visual form throughout the activities in *Sequencing Cut-Up Paragraphs*. They communicate in spoken form while participating in classroom discussions about the stories, while they communicate visually by pasting sentences in order and illustrating the sentences and stories in the activities.

4. **Students incorporate knowledge of language conventions (grammar, spelling, punctuation), media techniques, and genre to create and discuss a variety of print and nonprint texts.** Students use their knowledge of sentence structure and sequencing vocabulary cues to do the activities in this book.

────────────── NAEYC/IRA Position Statement Learning to Read and Write: ──────────────
Developmentally Appropriate Practices for Young Children

Each activity in this book supports one or more of the following recommended teaching practices for Kindergarten and Primary students:

1. **Teachers read to children daily and provide opportunities for students to independently read both fiction and nonfiction texts.** *Sequencing Cut-Up Paragraphs* contains 54 short fiction and nonfiction paragraphs for students to read, broken up into sentences so they can sequence them.

2. **Teachers provide opportunities for children to work in small groups.** The activities in *Sequencing Cut-Up Paragraphs* can easily be used with small groups.

3. **Teachers provide challenging instruction that expands children's knowledge of their world and expands vocabulary.** The paragraphs in *Sequencing Cut-Up Paragraphs* cover a wide variety of fiction and nonfiction topics, building students' vocabulary and background knowledge. In addition, the activities in this book specifically reinforce sequencing vocabulary.

4. **Teachers adapt teaching strategies based on the individual needs of a child.** The paragraphs in *Sequencing Cut-Up Paragraphs* are labeled according to reading level, so teachers can assign properly leveled activities to their students.

────────────────────── National Science Education Standards ──────────────────────

Several activities in this book support one or more of the following Life Science content standards for grades K-4:

1. **All students should understand the characteristics of organisms.** Several of the cut-up paragraphs in this book describe characteristics of different animals.

2. **All students should understand the life cycles of organisms.** One activity in this book includes information on the life cycle of the frog.

3. **All students should understand the relationship of organisms and environments.** Several of the cut-up paragraphs in this book describe the relationship between an organism and its environment.